Proud to Be Me!

Nicole Blais

Illustrated by Stef St.Denis

Proud to Be Me!
Copyright © 2020 by Nicole Blais

Tellwell Talent

www.tellwell.ca

ISBN

978-0-2288-2413-8 (Hardcover)

978-0-2288-2412-1 (Paperback)

978-0-2288-3204-1 (eBook)

For Deon, Mikayla and Ashton

I'm proud to be me,
For all the world to see,
For, you see...

I don't let the world
tell me who I should be!

Tall, thin, short, fat,
Happy, grumpy, slow, fast...

It's all good to me,
For I don't need to be you, and
you don't need to be me!

Unique and special is what we all are,
But the same we will never be...

So let's celebrate you,
And let's celebrate me!

Together, let's spread the good news,
That loving ourselves first should not be such a chore,

And trying to be like someone else,
Is most definitely a bore.

Burn bright like a shining star,
And appreciate others, for wherever they are,

We are all born for greatness,
And together we should be...

Proud to be you, and proud to be me!

CPSIA information can be obtained
at www.ICGtesting.com
Printed in the USA
LVHW072006040820
662398LV00036B/848